The Civilization of Love

> Humanity's next and biggest adventure is still ahead: building the Civilization of Love. People who believe in the power, beauty, and priority of love have a right and responsibility to put forward that agenda. We, the people of the earth, proclaim an end to the culture of death, the systems of exploitation and oppression, and commit our lives to building the Civilization of Love.

putting love first

Tony Bellizzi

the Civilization of Love

"Love and compassion are necessities, not luxuries. Without them humanity cannot survive." Dalai Lama

"A life without love is not worth living. So too, systems without love are not worth maintaining."
Tony Bellizzi

The Civilization of Love
Table of contents

The Greatest Adventure lies ahead
Defining Love
Love comes first
Civilization of Love Movement
The culture of death
The Illegitimacy
Living in the Civilization of Love
Understanding
The Final Frontier
Personal
Social
Political
Why hasn't it happened?
Leadership
Taking Action
Is it enough?
No Illusions
Epilogue

Special Thanks
Editor Shara Berkowitz

the Civilization of love

> *"Some day after we have mastered all the other forces in the world; we shall harness for God the energies of love. Then for the second time in the history of the world, man will have discovered fire."*   Teilhard de Chardin

The Greatest Adventure lies ahead

      This is not a major intellectual treatise, or a comprehensive collection of strategies for correcting a variety of things wrong with the world. The premise of this work is that the power of love makes all things new, and it is time we brought that principle into our shared collective lives through our institutions.
It is not enough to believe in love.
It is not enough to live your personal life with love.
What is needed is for people who believe in love to come together, and transform our organized, common life.
      As of now, there exists no group or political leaders standing for the priority of applying the ultimate power of love in the collective arena. While many of the sentiments expressed in this book have been expressed by individuals throughout human history, there remains no group that consistently promotes this Civilization of Love. Many people believe in love, are living it out to the best of their ability, and making a difference in the world through their families, communities, social or spiritual groups, and nations. Many people are committed to causes to fight against injustice and provide healing and opportunity. Any Civilization of Love surely starts with them.
      To continue to make these individual differences alone is not enough. We must ALSO work for the transformation of the larger institutions that govern the way we organize and interact with each other collectively. If we do not, we will continue the pattern of relegating the most important decisions to those who have no such commitment to love, but simply wield the greatest power, or are connected to those who do.

the Civilization of love

Nothing but disaster can ensue if you allow the people and systems who manage your shared reality operate by principles and practices that you personally would never engage in. Any excuse you can make for allowing this to occur is not worth the suffering and damage that will result. The corrupt, selfish, violent, petty, abusive, oppressive ways in which we conduct ourselves collectively disgraces us, and reveals our lack of imagination, courage, and integrity. Our collective human affairs are being conducted in ways that if applied to our own personal lives would lead to disaster. It is absurd to support this while hoping that somehow the worst possible outcomes will not occur.

> NEVER BE AFRAID TO RAISE YOUR VOICE FOR HONESTY AND TRUTH AND COMPASSION AGAINST INJUSTICE AND LYING AND GREED. IF PEOPLE ALL OVER THE WORLD...WOULD DO THIS, IT WOULD CHANGE THE EARTH.
> — WILLIAM FAULKNER

The truth is that we live in a way that shames us, in front of our children and in the judgment of history, and endangers future generations.

> "Insanity is doing the same thing over and over again and expecting different results." Einstein

There will always be those who will disregard, and even destroy any attempt to change the status quo. Others laugh at the prospect that human affairs be conducted in any way other than the law of the jungle, with occasionally a veneer of civilized behavior. They unwittingly serve the purposes of those who would like for all of us to fall asleep, withdraw into the pursuits of personal salvation, or erecting our own

the Civilization of love

manageable personal kingdoms in the face of slavery and oppression.

I have intentionally written this book avoiding religious perspective (separate pamphlets are available), because love is universal. Regardless of personal belief, there is a common ground that each of us holds within ourselves, a vision of how life on earth is supposed to be. The world should be a place of learning, loving, and creating, where growth occurs, life is appreciated and celebrated, troubles are faced together, and abundance shared; a world with far more light than darkness without unnecessary suffering, poverty, cruelty and loneliness. This vision is not a whimsical dream. No matter how much the world around us is in contradiction to it, the vision is no less true and real.

Life as lived on earth now is not as it could and should be, and this will always haunt you. You are not the only one.

The Urgency
The motivation for changing the world in such a huge way is the suffering of our fellow human beings who pay the price for our individual and collective refusal to love.
-people living with deep poverty, hunger, sickness.
-refugees, and all those suffering from war, genocide, and trafficking.
-people who lack the opportunity to work to provide basic necessities for themselves and their families, and can only survive my scavenging through waste and debris.
-the exploited, who because of oppression have no power, no voice
-those who suffer under the tyranny of violent zealots.
-everyone who suffers directly and indirectly from superficial systems that preach freedom, but ultimately enslave.

Yes, many people are living longer, and more comfortably than ever before. Yes, some diseases have been eradicated and a higher standard of living is now possible

the Civilization of love

for greater numbers than ever before, but at what price? Humanity suffers profound sickness resulting from a lack of love, and a soulless way of life.
*One out of three human beings is seriously depressed.
*One out of three human beings is addicted.

> "I am only one, but I am one. I cannot do everything, but I can do something. And because I cannot do everything, I will not refuse to do the something that I can do."
> — Edward Everett Hale

Everyday:
*36,000 children die of starvation and disease
*there are 42 armed conflicts
*thousands more are forced to enter refugee camps
*$1.7 trillion is spent annually on armaments instead of education and human needs
*there is a systematic rape and destruction of the earth in pursuit of profit
*statistics of inequality become increasingly staggering

This book and this movement are dedicated to everyone who struggles and suffers because there is not enough love in the world. Because the rest of us refuse to build "The Civilization of Love." the most vulnerable, the young and the poor, always pay the greatest price, and they are not expendable.

The Young
The errors of our ways are manifested in the youth of every culture. In the affluent world the development of the young is impeded by self-absorption and consumerism, drug abuse, social withdrawal, gang violence, suicide, self-harm, mindless mesmerization, and apathy. The young have distracted and amused to death. Modern life lacks

the Civilization of love

compelling goals that will capture their attention, harness their energy and lift their spirits.

In the developing world the dreams and talents of the young are denied through injustice and violence. Deep poverty and lack of resources means their energy is needed for the struggle to merely exist.

The materially poor

The grossest results of our refusal to love are revealed in the plight of our brothers and sisters struggling to eke out an existence in garbage dumps around the world, in the suffering bloated bodies of the starving and malnourished and diseased, in the dead bodies of those caught in wars over territory, resources, and drugs.

This book is written to speak to and reach into the heart of every human being who has been able to retain the spark of knowledge and hope that life as lived on the earth was meant to be so much better than it is. It's time for a new vision, a new way for humanity to envision itself and how we will go about living on this planet. It's time we committed to something that will give us dignity, motivate us to channel our energies, and bring us together. It's time to tell ourselves and our children a new story, one that will fashion a new and better way to see and understand our world, and determine the kind of world we build. It is time for a new narrative, one that reflects our values, behaviors, and lifestyles, molds our culture, laws, institutions, and social structures.

This new story is not new at all, it has just simply never been done. It is the Civilization of Love.

We have failed so far to make this world a home.

I did not come here to live like this.

I have a feeling you didn't either.

the Civilization of Love

> *Love is patient, love is kind. It does not envy, it does not boast, it is not proud. It does not dishonor others, it is not self-seeking, it is not easily angered, it keeps no record of wrongs. Love does not delight in evil but rejoices with the truth. It always protects, always trusts, always hopes, always perseveres. Love never fails.*
> 1Cor13:1-8

This new civilization exercises love's creativity to develop ways of living that demonstrate compassion and respect for the human race and for the world. Building the Civilization of Love is not just to restore what has been broken, but to create a brand new way of living together that will only be discovered as we refuse to indulge our fears and strike out boldly in love.

Human beings have tried an age of reason, an age of scientific and technological knowledge, discovery and advancement. Throughout history we have entertained the cults of personality, the attraction of clever propaganda, and blind allegiance to ideology. We have had an information age, convinced it would be enough. We have always worshiped at the altar of brute force and superior intelligence.

> *If I speak in the tongues of men or of angels, but do not have love, I am only a resounding gong or a clanging cymbal. If I have the gift of prophecy and can fathom all mysteries and all knowledge, and if I have a faith that can move mountains, but do not have love, I am nothing. If I give all I possess to the poor and give over my body to hardship that I may boast, but do not have love, I gain nothing.* 1Cor13

It has all been found lackluster at best, and horrific at worst. It is time for a new age of humanity, one in which reason, science, knowl-

the Civilization of love

edge, information and power are placed in the service of love, a Civilization of Love.
This is humanity's next and greatest adventure.

Defining love

While loving actions can often be stimulated by a feeling of affection, love is *not* sentimental emotion. Love is a choice, love is action. **Love is working for the good of another as much as you would for yourself.** Love is not merely following "the Golden Rule" treating others as you would want them to treat you. Love is working as hard to create good for others as much as you would for yourself. Civility and decency in human interactions is a minimal standard, transcendent love is a step beyond. It is possible, even though it often seems that we can't even treat each other civilly, never mind lovingly.

> *"Love does."*
> Bob Goff

> *"Compassion is not just feeling for someone, but seeking to change the situation. Love is demanding action."*
> Desmond Tutu

Cosmically, the unseen, but real actions of holding together (dark matter) and transcendence (dark energy), the qualities of love comprise almost all of the known universe. They are awesome and unstoppable. Transcendent, sacrificial love is the law of the universe, and therefore the only hope humanity ever has. Much closer to home, most of us can testify how the power of someone's unconditional loving action toward us transformed our own personal lives. Human life thrives when love guides our individual and collective lives. When human beings do not follow this law, the result is always disastrous destruction and suffering.

the Civilization of love

While affection is a driving force for us to create good for others, the force of love is beyond the warm and sentimental. It is personal and powerful. It is knowable, and yet beyond our limited comprehension. Nothing is more powerful than unconditional love, and so its use requires courage to move beyond the fear-driven needs of the ego. Because of the inherent presence of fear-based resistance within individuals and systems, there is an inescapable sacrificial dimension to the loving act.

Love comes first

The truth about the primacy of love; may or may not be reinforced during the course of a human lifetime by parents, family, spiritual and social teachers and leaders, literature, music, and art, but it always lies in the inner voice of conscience in the deepest part of the heart and soul.

> *"One's philosophy is not best expressed in words; it is expressed in the choices one makes... and the choices we make are ultimately our responsibility."*
> Eleanor Roosevelt

The truth is always the same:
> ***"Love is the answer;***
> ***no matter what is the question."***

Love alone is the purpose, motivation, and fruit of all truly human activity.

Perhaps you've striven your whole life to life by this code, and you've wanted to see the world operate by it as well. Meanwhile you've watched things heartbreakingly deteriorate. Throughout all of human history, people everywhere see the highest ideals of their society fall by the wayside when people of power, unwilling to control their own greed, corrupt governments, institutions, and systems, and violate every sense of decency and justice. The time has come (in fact it is long overdue) for a new

the Civilization of love

paradigm of how humans can see ourselves, individually behave, and collectively conduct our affairs as a species.

The Civilization of Love movement

The Civilization of Love is an international movement proclaiming and living the primacy of love in all human activity; building a planetary culture based on the universal law of love as opposed to the law of the jungle. It is a global movement of people aligning themselves with the highest principles human beings hold, willing to risk conducting their lives in a loving, compassionate way and challenging their leaders to lead with those same standards.

The Civilization of Love movement:
* Love must be the guiding principle for all laws and actions taken by individual states and collective unions.
* Our collective affairs must be run by the same principles and practices of love that we aspire to in our personal lives.

1- Proposes that human beings live their individual and collective lives guided by the primacy of love, rejecting whatever is not "love-based."

2- Affirms, encourages, and empowers ways of living communally that give honor and dignity to human life, transform institutions, and relieve the suffering that results from an individually and collectively held fear-based paradigm.

It is not a new or original concept that human beings should live individual and collective lives motivated and animated by love, giving expression to their ultimate unity. What **would be new** is a global movement guided by these simple principles that is proposing and prepared to establish a world shaped by these principles:

the Civilization of love

* Love is more important than anything else.
* Change starts within the individual, and flows out into society.
* Love can and should be the center of collective life, the foundation of all human personal and collective interaction.
* People have a right to determine that their collective systems be governed by the highest principles of loving by which they live their personal lives.

> *What does it matter how efficiently you have have organized your world if you have put it all together for the wrong purpose?*

      To place at the center, that all human activity must be for the good of everyone, IS simple; but not easy. The implementation of the Civilization of Love agenda will be incredibly complex, the most challenging task humanity has ever faced. In every society this cause requires the involvement of citizens who see the bigger picture being committed to the process of loving transformation and creating a Civilization of Love within their own society and among the entire human family.

      Throughout human history, many have spoken about love, and countless individuals have lived their lives according to principles of love, kindness and compassion. This will remain forever the way humans are meant to live. Life-giving love is meant to be the foundation of the human institutions of marriage and the family. Human institutions have sprung up over the course of history to lovingly aid in the lifting up of fellow human beings, and

> *"Love is a force more formidable than any other. It is invisible - it cannot be seen or measured, yet it is powerful enough to transform you in a moment, and offer you more joy than any material possession could."*
> — Barbara de Angelis

the Civilization of love

providing assistance and relief to those in need. True religions and spiritual institutions promote a more loving way of life. Countless numbers of human beings have dreamed that one day love would be the way that humans live together. The only reasonable response to life is to love. Because we are all ultimately connected, love really is the law.

Proclaiming the Civilization of love

The Civilization of Love already exists in the hearts, minds, and souls of humanity. It already exists everyday through individual and communal selfless loving acts of compassion and solidarity. The beauty of life is that no one need wait for anyone else to wake up, in order to live a life of loving. We don't transform society so that we might then become able to love. We love, even if no one else wants to join us, appreciate what we are are doing, or return our love. True love has nothing to do with the response of others.

The Civilization of Love movement is about additionally transforming our collective life so that our unified efforts reflect and express love as well. When will the Civilization of Love be manifested as the dominant way we live out our collective lives on this planet? Whenever a generation has the moral courage and stamina to discard the current fear-based system.

There is no good reason that the future must simply be an extension or expansion of what we have today, which shows us that despite:
* technological and scientific advances
* the unprecedented proliferation of information
* the highest level of comfort and affluence the world has ever seen

the **quality** of life does **not** necessarily improve.

the Civilization of love

The key ingredient determining the quality of all human life is the presence, or lack of love. We intuitively know this truth, and many of us attempt to live it out in our personal lives to the best of our ability. And yet, when it comes to our social, political, economic, and sometimes even religious institutions, we allow leaders to govern according to a fear-based code. A life without love is not worth living. So too, systems without love are not worth maintaining.

"He killed my ma. He killed my pa. I'll vote for HIM." This disturbing campaign slogan for President Charles Taylor in Liberia is a most extreme expression of how, even though leaders may inflict horrific suffering, people can be manipulated, and terrified to stand against that abusive power. People are afraid that if they stop supporting this fear-driven system and the illegitimate power-brokers who benefit from it, chaos will ensue. Inertia, fear of danger and uncertainty, and avoidance of the uncomfortable keep people aligned with the familiar, as defective as it might be. The unknown could be worse. And how else would humanity proceed? Love-based, rather than fear-based options are never offered.

While some leaders employ brute force to maintain their position, other leaders manipulate their constituency's hope for a better way forward. All too often their conscience, and their consciousness is limited to, and driven by the fear-based, corrupt systems that cultivated them and real change never comes. As Einstein said: *"Problems cannot be solved within the consciousness that created them."*

Humanity is standing at a crossroads. The Civilization of Love movement is crucial because the ultimate climax of the loveless system is increasing chaos and violence. The "perfect storm" of terrorist groups, mass

the Civilization of Love

medication, corporate and financial greed, wanton violence, media manipulation, increased social, environmental, and personal stresses, the pump is being primed. The world is well into the process of establishing levels of fascism that humanity has not seen in some time, and probably more severe than have ever proliferated. The terror created by those who wish only to kill and destroy is real. The powerless, guided by the violent, create chaotic destruction; which in turn serves the needs of the powerful who strike up the chorus calling for greater order, manipulating the masses to cry out for the enslavement that might protect from the terror. People are being groomed to cry out for their own chains.

    Calling for the creation of a Civilization of Love is not a naive assumption that if world leaders will just behave themselves and do the right thing, somehow there will be world peace. Patterns of love are first received and present in human hearts. They are then cultivated by and spread out into family and significant personal relationships. From there the extension is out into communities, the larger society, and the world. The way to the change we want to see, is through the personal involvement of those who have the awareness that love is the way. It comes through their acceptance of personal responsibility for creating something new wherever they have been planted.

> "Our human compassion binds us the one to the other - not in pity or patronizingly, but as human beings who have learnt how to turn our common suffering into hope for the future."
> Nelson Mandela

    The emphasis of the Civilization of Love movement is that love be both the foundation and at the forefront of all human progress. Individual issues must con-

the Civilization of love

tinue to be addressed, and action taken. Yet the power and energy for change can be diminished when splintered among diverse competing causes. The momentum for change can become fragmented and human energy exhausted by countless groups focused on addressing endless concerns. No one issue is more important than love; because without love, solutions only bring about the creation of new troubles.

No challenge that humanity is facing now or will face in the future should ever be approached without love.

The goals of the Civilization of Love movement are:
1- To affirm and encourage those who already know the truth about the primacy of love.
2- To energize and empower those who, up until now, have been reluctant to take action.
3- To awaken and enlighten those for whom this is a new concept.
4- To transform life on the earth for future generations through personal and collective action, and the renewal of all human institutions.

The Civilization of Love movement is:
*supportive- fostering community among change agents
*systemic- working for institutional transformation
*structured- establishing and implementing specific
   goals and plans
*spontaneous- growing and renewing constantly
*sustained- evaluating constantly and rededicating

the Civilization of love

The Civilization of Love movement is:

Global
People of every nation regardless of economic status, political inclination, religious belief, age, or social outlook, stepping up to assume personal responsibility for creating a better way of living, including assuming leadership in moving their own group, organization, society, and nation state in the practice of loving discourse and action.

Comprehensive
Supporting specific initiatives to improve the quality of life for human beings, but going beyond niche issues.

Compassionate
Only strategies and practices that address, include, and lift up the most vulnerable members of humanity are valid.

Courageous
The movement is about Imaging and building a brave new world. Brave because of:

*The raw courage it will take to challenge the status quo that has been so painstakingly built, and deal with the consequences of that.

*The risk of operating from the level of consciousness needed for its implementation, and the price paid at the hands of those not aligned in that way.

*The great personal sacrifice and social ostracism that can come from the refusal to adhere to the belief that the best humanity can aspire to is fear-based law of the jungle with at best a civilized veneer.

the Civilization of Love

Especially, in societies where violence in all its forms is accepted and justified, these ideals deserve to be articulated and need to be brought into play. Again, the Civilization of Love is not a new concept. All throughout history there have been voices that have lamented the sad state of human affairs; and dreamed of a better way of life, one worthy of the dignity of human beings.

Love:	
Creates	not destroys
Shares	not exploits
Frees	not enslaves
Protects	not oppresses

Conducting individual, and collective lives on fear-based beliefs and practices has been tried and failed horribly. The change that humanity is crying out for in society after society, will not be found by simply changing the faces of those in power. What is needed is a new consciousness; one committed to the loving protection and compassionate development of all. Some will say this is a delusional belief. On the contrary, **the *delusion* is believing and expecting that the collective whole would be exempt from the same effects experienced when we violate of the law of love in our personal lives.**

With full awareness of the obstacles that lay ahead in the implementation of the Civilization of Love, we commit ourselves to working for this better way, knowing full well that violence, whether it be military, economic, or social is always the last refuge of the fearful and unimaginative. We will not muddle through one disaster after another, seeing each other as enemy and accepting the fear-mongering propaganda. We owe this to our children. We can be the generation that stood up and said: "no more".

The bottom line is that there is no culture, society or government on earth now, or ever, that has used the principle and practice of love as their social narrative,

the Civilization of Love

their guiding force. There have been societies that have held to spiritual or religious principles; but in practice conducted wars and other forms of violence and social manipulation that go directly against those same principles. Simply no people on earth can say "we tried this. It doesn't work."

The Culture of Death

We do not live right on this planet, and to allow this to continue is to shame ourselves before our children, subsequent generations, and all of human history. To turn away, and not face this reality and its consequences, is to shame ourselves further. Yes, it is true that strides have been made in science, health and education. The development of technology and eradication of many diseases are impressive displays of human ingenuity. Thankfully we still have enough of our humanity intact that we rally when there is a natural disaster. What we do not address, and what escapes our attention and lacks our compassion, is the effort needed to alleviate the effects of the daily catastrophic aspects of life on earth that lead to untold oppression, suffering, death, and destruction. We are too willing to go along with systems and ways of doing things that lack love and in most cases, justice.

If it is true that something can be defined by its opposite, then the state of the world offers an incredible clarity of what the Civilization of Love would look like. The world is rapidly becoming an increasingly loveless place. Forms and degrees of violence, hatred, destruction, enslavement, oppression, exploitation, selfishness, and greed, many of which could never have been

> "Sometimes I wonder whether the world is being run by smart people who are putting us on, or by imbeciles who really mean it."   Mark Twain

the Civilization of Love

foreseen years ago, have taken hold and multiplied, systematically destroying human beings, and their home.

> *The order in the world that is founded on love builds societies that are free and prosperous. The counterfeit order of the culture of death brings only bondage, suffering and poverty. and institutional evil, such as slavery, corporate corruption, and caste systems.* — Darrow

When love is absent, death and destruction will flourish. Where selfish, greedy, and violent fear-based ideas are practiced and allowed to dominate, no culture of any value can develop. The Civilization of Love is not a collection of bandaids for fixing one crisis at a time. It results from a systematic application of the love ingrained in every human heart and soul to every challenge, and to the work of every social, economic, educational, religious, and political institution.

For some time now, the current era in human history has been described by many as a "culture of death." It is the name given to the collective nightmare threatening humanity and its home. Intelligent, enlightened, compassionate human beings can see that life as lived on this planet at this time cannot possibly be the best we are capable of. Whether you attribute this deficiency and decay to the interference of love-resistant, malevolent multidimensional spiritual entities or alien beings, the human tendency and capacity for aggression and instinctual survival at any cost, conspiracies of the elite, human inertia, stupidity and weakness, or all of the above, the reality is the same: we are living individual and collective lives that range from beneath our dignity at best, to a living hell, at worst.

the Civilization of Love

Humans are either struggling with every bit of their energy to survive as they always have throughout all of human history, or in places of affluence raising new generations who are bored, medicating themselves to numb their sense of purposeless and uselessness in a system that devours. There are so many ways the culture of death devours people. No matter what you believe about how we got here, what is clear is that the "culture of death" has no respect for human life and destroys human beings.

Information about everything that is wrong with this world is readily available. The cumulative picture of a disintegrating civilization is a *"Culture of Death"*.

Lies

At the foundation of the Culture of Death is a combination of animalistic drives, and the propagation of a fear based multitude of lies. The foundation of all other lies is the falsehood that we are not connected to each other, and that society, our collective life, and our entire world can function without concern for one another.

Additional lies include:
- consumption is the expression of success and increases happiness and wellbeing
- the resources necessary for human life are inexhaustible
- only the strongest deserve to survive
- if we all mind our own business, trust the people in charge, and just take care of ourselves, everything will be just fine
- political solutions alone, without changes of heart and personal behavior, can bring about lasting peace
- adherence to ideology can bring order and peace of mind
- greater speed brings better results and a better life
- life ultimately has no purpose or meaning
- personal pleasure, comfort, and security are the sole purpose of life

the Civilization of love

Increased fear, manifested as violence and greed, fuels the Culture of Death. The systematic enslavement and suffering of human beings, and the raping of the planet are increasing at a staggeringly rapid rate.
Without the driving force of love to guide them, human beings fall into **two forms of greed** and battle each other:
1-Those who want more than they need, and have the potential to oppress, exploit, kill in order to obtain and keep whatever they want
2- Those who want something for nothing, and either through theft or manipulation, attempt to gain what is not rightfully theirs because they did not work for it.

The greed for more than we need, or for what belongs to others, is satiated by some through established, accepted organs of society, and systemic violence. Others implement their greed through their own systems of terrorism and crime. Our world, our collective life, is crumbling under the weight of fear, expressed as selfishness and greed. The appetite for unlimited money, power and resources at all costs brings down any person, any social organism.

The Culture of Death
The Tyranny of Exploitation and Oppression
The Systematic enslavement of human beings through disorder and the loss of human freedom:
-systematic legislated erosion of freedom and rights
-surveillance and the end of privacy
-rape, torture, child abuse, molestation
-human trafficking and slavery

> *Suffering is present in the world in order to release love, in order to give birth to works of love towards neighbor, in order to transform the whole of human civilization into a "civilization of love".*
> St. John Paul II

the Civilization of love

-refugee crisis
-consolidation of and restricted availability of information through corporate domination of media
-increased incarceration rates

The Murder of human beings
-the elimination of all who are not useful: unborn, the poor, the aged, the weak, sick and unproductive
-proliferation of war, militarism, terrorism, and violence
-vast proliferation of the military industrial complex
-rise of violent extremist groups
-religious tyranny
-child soldiers
-euthanasia
-genocides
-death penalty

> *War is a soulless void. War is barbarity, perversion and pain. Human decency and tenderness are crushed. All human beings become objects, pawns to use or kill. Wars may have to be fought to ensure survival, but they are always tragic. They always bring to the surface the worst elements of any society, those who have a penchant for violence and a lust for absolute power. War as a human enterprise is a matter of sin. It is a firm of hatred for one's fellow human beings. War's essence is death, and is always morally depraved. there are times when a nation is pushed into a war. But this violence always deforms and maims those who use it."* Chris Hedges

-intentional termination of 1 in 4 pregnancies
-wanton murder and aggressive violence of criminals, the deranged, gangs, religious fanatics, and drug cartels

The Destruction of the earth
-degradation of the environment through pollution of the air, land, and water
-destruction of the oceans and the water supply
-damages from mining of energy sources
-loss of rights to basic resources such as clean air and water

> *"The earth, our home, is beginning to look more and more like an immense pile of filth."* Pope Francis.

the Civilization of love

-proliferation of GMOs, contamination of food with pesticides, antibiotics and steroids, and methods that destroy the nutritional value of food
-destruction of forests
-wasting of resources

Deprivation, Poverty
-world hunger and disease
-36,000 children deaths daily,
-12 million live on the brink of starvation
-failure to provide security for the young and most vulnerable

   * In the USA, the richest country on earth, 1 in 7 people live in poverty. In 2012 over 46.2 million, the highest number in 53 years of measuring poverty 15% of all Americans, and 22% of all children.

Economic Injustice and exploitation
-consumer societies cultivate self-indulgence, insatiable appetites for consumption, and indifference to consequences.
-tribal and systemic unchecked personal, government, institutional, and corporate greed and corruption
-skewed distribution of resources
-loss of livelihoods and opportunities to earn a decent living as human labor is devalued by globalization and technology
-agribusiness wiping out small farmers, contaminating food with pesticides, antibiotics and steroids. (The subjugation of the land, which started with native peoples, now includes local farmers and fishermen.)
-privatization of essential resources, surrender to corporate interests
-increased income disparity and consolidation of wealth as strengthened interlocking systems give advantage to the few at the expense of the many

the Civilization of love

*1/6 of the world's population lives on less than $1.00 a day, 162 million of then on less than 50 cents a day.

Dehumanization
The loss of human dignity
-moral decay and personal psychological disintegration
-increasing disrespect for and expendability of human life, as the worth of human beings is determined by the market
-behavioral addictions including gambling, gaming, technology
-substance addictions including drugs and alcohol
-mass medication of society through the proliferation of legal and illegal drugs
-the persistence of sexism, racism, religious intolerance
-mesmerization of masses through consumption of mindless entertainment and unprecedented diversions and distractions, cults of celebrity
-objectification of the human body
-proliferation of materialism, consumerism; consumption turned into a compulsion
-withdrawal of masses from participation in human affairs
-image based politics and economics; voting and buying into propaganda based on emotion, focusing on presentation and performance rather than truth

The Division
-polarization, hatred, racism, discrimination
-increasing lack of civility in human discourse
-demonization of opponents and promotion of fear and sus-

> "People have institutionalized oppressive power in the form of surrender." Ralph Nader

> "when a population becomes distracted by trivia, when a cultural life is redefined as a perpetual round of entertainments, when serious public conversation becomes a form of baby talk, when it, in short, a people become an audience and their public business a vaudeville act, then a nation finds itself at risk; culture death is a clear possibility." Neil Postman

the Civilization of love

picion
-breakdown of marriage and family life

The Culture of Death is marked by deadly extremes:
- death by hunger and malnutrition — obesity
- powerlessness — corruption
- inability to conceive — termination of 1 in 4 pregnancies
- poverty — over-consumption

The accumulation of these realities has resulted in a "perfect storm" of destruction of whatever is good about human life.

The side effects of this perfect storm
- apathy
- social isolation
- depression
- addiction
- homicide
- hopelessness
- fear and anxiety
- loss of intimacy
- conformity
- suicide
- self-destruction of the young
- relativism
- powerlessness, denial of possibility systemic change
- loss of personal responsibility for health
- passivity and technological stimulus mesmerization
- loss of belief in and connection to transcendent love
- infantilization and inability to act responsibly
- instant gratification, resulting in the loss of character that comes from having to wait
- medication of society with 1 in 5 adults on medication for anxiety and depression
- the blind pursuit of power, fame and fortune at any cost destroying the quality of personal and collective life

the Civilization of love

There are basic truths that cannot be ignored without tremendous peril:
*When you allow so many of your species to suffer from deprivation, you can never have true abundance.
* When you kill babies, the most vulnerable human lives, you can never have true security.
* When you treat you oceans and waterways like toilets, and garbage dumps you can never insure the essentials needed for basic life.
* When you protect the powerfully violent and corrupt from real consequences, you can never have true justice.
* When you reward greed you can never reap the countless fruits of a moral society.
* When you medicate the masses, you can never thrive creatively or energetically.
* When you promote self-indulgence, self-gratification and self-absorption you can never marshall the resources needed to preserve your way of life.
* When you allow basic human needs like water and seeds to be sold, your society can never be sustainable.
* When you allow countless forms of slavery, you can throw around the word freedom, and wave a flag all you want, your people are dying, literally and soulfully.

    We are clearly sickened, damaged and bored by the alternative to a loving way of life. Our responses range from hatred, killing, and oppressing, to escaping into drugs, other addictions, depression, or diversions of choice. When we add up all the efforts to distract ourselves, to remove ourselves from reality: addiction, suicide, fanatical religion, medication, obsession with sports and entertainment, virtual reality, social withdrawal to name a few, clearly large numbers of human beings don't want to be here. The question remains: will we allow the

the Civilization of love

consequences of this cumulative painful, mediocre, and disgusting culture to be enough motivation to take drastic action, or will we yawn, and go back to flipping channels and checking our social media one more time?
***Because until we are truly motivated, we will do nothing. Love is not emotion, but it is fueled by emotion. Can we, will we, allow our hurt, disappointment, sadness, anger, frustration, and outrage to move us out of our complacency and fear, and affect the change we know is needed?

The Illegitimacy

It is time to tell the truth about the designers, promoters, instruments and sustainers of the Culture of Death:

Religious and Spiritual groups and Institutions

-Any religion that conducts, promotes or does not forcefully oppose the killing, mistreatment, hatred, or discrimination against those who believe differently from them is an inauthentic religion. Any religious leader who does so is illegitimate. Militaristic, terroristic violence in the name of religious propagation is inherently evil and evidently contradictory to any true religion.

-Any religious or spiritual group which exists strictly for their own maintenance, to the neglect (this includes lip service and token efforts) of true service to others is a fraud.

-Any spiritual teaching, practice or path that focuses only on personal salvation, and individual benefits, leading to a withdrawal from engaging in and lovingly transforming reality to the neglect of loving action on behalf of others is inauthentic and is not a true spiritual path.

Political and Economic Institutions

-Any government that uses its laws and institutional apparatus strictly for the benefit of the few to the neglect of the many within its society is illegitimate.

the Civilization of love

-Any government that does not insure that economic entities (banks, corporations, financial institutions) serve the common good, and allows them to pursue their own profits at any cost, to the detriment of the common good is not a valid government.

-Any government that takes human life and/or sanctions the taking of human life, at any and all stages of life, in their own society or any other, is murderous and illegitimate.

-Any national government that functions for the benefit for their own people at the expense of other nations, operates out of a limited vision, and is illegitimate.

-Any society that leaves it's debts to the next generation to pay, shames itself, and is unworthy of whatever they have been able to accumulate.

-Any government or organization that cares only about their own continuation, and does not operate with concern for the greater good is deficient and illegitimate.

Social and Educational Institutions

-Any society that does not prioritize the safety, thorough education, development and preparation of the young is criminally negligent and well on the path of collapse.

-Any society that does not strive for equal educational opportunity for all it's young is elitist and invalid.

-Any educational institution or system that does not develop the total student, or prepare them to live in and lead society according to a code of decency is defective, and must transformed, or dismantled and replaced.

Inept or oppressive leadership

-Any leader who uses their position of power for their own benefit, or the benefit of their select associates and/or group(s) they represent, or who uses their power to harm individuals and/or groups of people is criminally illegitimate.

the Civilization of love

-Any leader who accepts and corroborates with the trappings and privileges of power is not authentic.
-Any leader willing to send their young to kill on their behalf in illegitimate.
-Any human system controlled by individuals and groups of individuals, utilizing their positions only to insure the maintenance of their personal power and position is illegitimate.
   **And people of integrity, committed to love,
   do not allow them to run things.**

   The perpetrators and sustainers of the Culture of Death, whether out of evil or ignorance, like everyone else, must be loved, and they must also be stopped. The loving action is refusing to allow them to continue their actions, which enslave and harm others and disgrace themselves, the institutions they lead, and the people they are meant to represent, lead, and serve.
From the perspective of love, certain things are seen as unacceptable, even horrific:
-allowing another to starve, while wasting food personally is unconscionable
-not acting in the face of injustice and human suffering is inhumane
-killing a baby is an incomprehensible evil
-passing on fear-based prejudices and hatreds to the next generation is deplorable

The purpose of this movement is to speak truth to power and organize for structural change, and not to employ victim-like mentality behavior of seeking out and punishing an "enemy" who is the reason for our unhappiness or suffering. Illegitimate leaders must be stopped, not hated.

the Civilization of Love

The acquiescing of the culture of death leads to hopeless despair, self-destruction, and even crying out for the safety of chains.
We don't have to.
We can love.

> *"The ultimate weakness of violence is that it is a descending spiral, begetting the very thing it seeks to destroy. Instead of diminishing evil, it multiplies it. Through violence you may murder the liar, but you cannot murder the lie, nor establish the truth. Through violence you murder the hater, but you do not murder the hate. In fact, violence merely increases hate ... Returning violence for violence multiples violence, adding deeper darkness to a night already devoid of stars. Darkness cannot drive out darkness; only light can do that. Hate cannot drive out hate: only love can do that."* — Martin Luther King Jr.

Living in the Civilization of Love

We can know what the Civilization of Love looks like by examining The Culture of Death. By seeing clearly the foundation of fear and lies, leading to practices that destroy the earth and human beings on it, carried out by illegitimate leaders, we can know exactly what we must and must not do.

> *"We are put on this earth for a little space that we may learn to bear the beams of love."* — William Blake

The Civilization of Love requires a radical shift and the creation of something new. We cannot, we dare not, accept this Culture of Death and do nothing, or worse yet, foolishly hope that someone with a fear-based level of consciousness, might somehow miraculously lead us to a promised land.
The Civilization of Love looks the way love does: bold, creative, intelligent, passionate, joyful, extravagant, self-

the Civilization of love

sacrificing, powerful, and infinite. Love fulfills the potential for good and purifies what is evil. Every person we meet, in every situation, in any given moment we will ever live in, is either alive in love, or in need of love.

> "What love we've given, we'll have forever. What love we fail to give, will be lost for all eternity."
> Leo Buscaglia

Whether you believe that things have become so far gone that only a deity can save us, or that human beings can turn this around, or that it is a combination of the two, the reality is the same: we must do something.

The Civilization of Love is a movement, and that implies movement, action, by those motivated to act. Utilizing and transforming existing structures, and creating new ones when necessary, we serve and work for the protection and proliferation of light and love on the earth. Together people, and eventually nations, committed to the centrality of love in human affairs, create a dynamism that individuals and groups not yet committed to the community of love will be attracted to. There will be an excitement, a synergy that will rise out of the sacrifices of those who are willing to be on the frontier of loving engagement.

Human history, on the deepest level, is the story of the Civilization of Love trying to break out in the face of the proliferation of the Culture of Death. It is the battle between a system where people are judged by, and used for their social and economic value; and a way of living that respects and cultivates human dignity. When the policies and actions of the people that run the system are guided by animalistic violence in all its forms, strengthened in and justified by their fear-based propaganda, they jeopardize the wellbeing of everyone, and put eve-

the Civilization of love

ryone's safety at risk. For those who know the truth about the primacy of love, it is simply irresponsible to allow this go occur, and we cannot do so any longer without sustaining catastrophic damage.

There are great risks inherent in building a Civilization of Love; but those risks are far outweighed by the dangers of a world dominated by fearful individuals, fear-mongering illegitimate leaders, and their media mouthpieces, strengthening tribal and organized selfishness, greed, and hatred.

What's riskier: taking a chance on love *or* hoping against hope that continuing the spiral down the black hole of the Culture of Death will still somehow leave intact for future generations a world and a way of life with some semblance of goodness and humanity?

All institutions are meant to reflect love and the highest values of our human heritage, by expressing, encouraging, and empowering through their policies and activity the best in humanity rather than rewarding the most base of instincts: fear-based greed and violence. Dismantling the culture of death, by withdrawing from it and refusing to give it energy is only the first step. The real adventure and challenge comes with building what must replace it. Vigilance is needed to insure that the process not be taken over by those who will attempt to poison, discredit, and destroy the Civilization of Love movement, causing humanity to regret ever overthrowing the enslavement and making us cry out for it even more.

Guiding principles of the Civilization of Love
* Human Solidarity is central- *"we walk beside"*
* There are Basic civil liberties:
    -to life

the Civilization of love

 -to believe what you want
 -to express what you believe
 -to gather with whom you want
 -to be protected under law and due process
* Children, not just some children, **all children** are the number one priority for parents and for our entire species. They are provided with their basic needs, education, and the opportunity to develop and contribute their gifts.
* The sacredness of life and the dignity of the human person is the foundation of a society, and the measure of every institution is whether it threatens or enhances them. States will not directly kill or sanction the taking of human life in any form.
* Marriage and the family are respected as the central social institutions and are supported and strengthened, not undermined. Married people are faithful to each other and self-sacrificing for their children.
* There is enforcement against Illegal, murderous activity such as genocide, economic warfare, abuse, human trafficking, and slavery in all its forms.
* There is a monumental sustained effort to eradicate hunger, disease and poverty, so they will be forever relegated to the tragic dustbins of history, as the tragic vestiges of a less enlightened age. The deepening divisions between rich and poor, is ended by putting the needs of the poor and vulnerable and the middle classes first, ahead of the desires of the rich.
* War and violence are rejected as an legitimate methods of conflict resolution, and new structures and methods are put in place to resolve conflicts by peaceful means.
* Governments and social insti-

> "The vain effort to purify the world through force is always self-defeating. Those who insist that the world can be molded into their vision are the most susceptible to violence as antidote."
> Chris Hedges

the Civilization of love

tutions operate with compassionate vision, integrity, transparency, wide consultation, and collaboration to create a loving world, with dignity for all human beings.
* Humanity assumes responsibility for the care for and protection of the environment, stewardship of the earth for future generations. There is a reversal of any current policies and practices that lead to the destruction of the environment leading to an eventual end to the pollution of the air, water, and land. Basic essentials for life such as air, water, and seeds are protected as human rights and not controlled by private corporations.
* All human beings are valued above material things, loved and respected. Social relationships are guided by integrity, not usefulness to any economic machine.
* The world's resources are shared, with special respect to the people whose land contains the resources.
* Refugees are restored to their homelands.
* Transparency and legal consequences eliminate corruption and oppression.
* Illegitimate, corrupt leaders are removed. Unjust government systems dismantled.
* People exercise their right and duty to participate in society, seeking together the common good and well-being of all, especially the vulnerable and those most in need.
* The steady erosion of freedom is reversed and human rights are protected, including the fundamental rights to life and the opportunity to work for providing the basics for human living.
* Citizens live out their duties and responsibilities to each other, their families, and the larger society, and work for justice, peace and healing.
* The dignity of work is recognized and the rights of workers is respected. Individuals are the providers for their families. Government's job is to insure that the playing

the Civilization of love

field is level for opportunity for all its citizens. Economies serve the people, and not the other way around. Corporations and banks are accountable to the people and their governments. The dignity of workers is protected by their basic rights being respected: the rights to productive work, to decent and fair wages, to organize, to private property, and to economic initiative.
* There is a solidarity among humans, recognizing the unity of the human family regardless of national, racial, ethnic, economic, and ideological differences. All people are treated as members of the same family. Racism and discrimination are not tolerated.
* There is real discussion and significant change on issues of injustice on a global scale.

Understanding

Empires, be they European, Chinese, American, Islamic, or Russian, attain their status and their wealth through the exploitation of the less powerful. Who does the earth belong to? Does the land and everything on it and under it belong to the people who happen to live on that particular piece of it, or to the people powerful enough to take it from the people who live on it? Or does it belong to everyone? And if so, how will that be governed? As always, societies, organizations and the entire human family will continuously have to hammer out details and make decisions on how to answer major questions like these and proceed forward. In the Civilization of Love the difference will be that every law and action be decided upon by the criteria of: **will it bring into being the greatest amount of love?** All challenges to, and protests against policies will have a single demand: **"Where is the love?"**

the Civilization of Love

The Civilization of Love is not a restoration of some bygone era, simply because what it is has never been carried out before on any national or international stage. There may have been times in history that were more calm, or less corrupt, when people behaved themselves better than other times; but The Civilization of Love has never been attempted. Why?

There is no shortage of reasons. Before anyone is tempted to blame or punish anyone else or their systems for their failures, it is helpful to remember how far away each of us in our personal lives is from living out pure, unconditional love.

We need to understand and admit, but not limit ourselves to:
*our own personal fear-based human nature.
*the entrenchment of earlier thought patterns and the results of previously made decisions.
*inertia: the resistance to change in every person and system of human organization.

Simply put:
*It's hard to do (violence is easier)
*There are countless obstacles
  (it's just human nature and entrenched patterns)
*Most people around you are not living it (why make enemies?)

The Final Frontier

The Civilization of Love starts with a change in the heart and soul of the human person, and flows out from there into their personal lives. Attitude and vision have to change first, accompanied by a commitment to change. The Civilization of Love can exist wherever we are present, and love can flow with whomever we may be interacting with. Someone can experience living in the Civilization of Love in your presence.

the Civilization of love

The Civilization of Love extends from within you. It ripples out into your family, your school or workplace; from there out into your geographical, virtual and spiritual communities; from there out into your nation and into the entire world, and even into the universe. There is no such thing as an insignificant or wasted act of love. Each affects the entire reality.

The incubator of the civilization of love is marriage and the family. Parents and families are the fundamental building blocks, the primary builders of the Civilization of Love. They either cultivate or destroy in their children the instinct to love.

> *"Love is the only force capable of transforming an enemy into friend."*
> Martin Luther King Jr.

Pillars of the Civilization of Love
A Culture of Compassion

Many reading up to now are attracted to the idea that things must change, that love is the way to live, and that it is not only not unreasonable but morally compelling that social institutions and collective life also be governed by love, and that leaders who cannot recognize this need to go.

These are the qualities of love that are required for any real change to occur. They are qualities that are enormously difficult to cultivate and express within us personally, and even harder to enact in groups. This message may be unattractive, but no real change can occur without the transformation resulting from these qualities.

Pillars of the Civilization of Love		A Culture of Compassion	
Humility	Mercy	Passion	Dignity
Sacrifice	Empathy	Perseverance	Integrity
Generosity	Forgiveness	Creativity	Engagement
Communication	Reconciliation	Joy	Respect
Service	Gratitude	Courage	Solidarity

the Civilization of love

Any family, group, organization, society, nation or species society that cultivates these pillars is strong in its foundation, and the fruits are peace, order, truth, beauty, and freedom expressed as:
Community   Healing   Creative service   Justice

By working to make compassion the new norm, we are refusing to give energy to any loveless system of oppression and exploitation:
*When choices have to be made we refuse to settle for leaders who do not have love as the foundation of their platform.
*When organizing is needed, we form groups committed to building the Civilization of Love.
*When resistance is necessary we peacefully, and creatively stand up.
*When we are belittled and beaten, we shake it off and move forward.

     Some will rail against this Civilization of Love, saying it is foolish naive dreaming, and can never be attained. **What matters** is not the perfect attainment of this goal, it **is the change that will occur in humanity** as we more intensely and collectively pursue something so beautiful and so powerful on such a large scale that has never been attempted before. Our focus is more on the journey than the destination.

The Civilization of Love movement is personal

     Not merely standing *against* the culture of death, as individuals, and together we stand *for* the Civilization of Love. We do so not though fear, guilt and shame, but with joy, courage and beauty. We don't just rage against

the Civilization of love

the darkness, we light a candle of hope. We radiate The Civilization of Love through our being and we build it through the actions of our lives. In countless ways we tell a better story that awakens the better story in others. We lead by the way we live what we believe, a way of life, faithful in the small things, that acknowledges the dignity and worth of every person, that manifests mercy, compassion and justice for all, especially the marginalized, poor, forsaken, and forgotten.

We all have a desire to be free to do what is right, and overcome our own inertia and fear, to live and love generously. Fighting for justice, making right what is wrong, demands a personal cost, paying a price. It means leaving behind our comforts and making a lifelong commitment. The grand gesture is too simple. Change is messy. Standing with the vulnerable is inconvenient and even painful, but ideas mean nothing without action.

The Civilization of Love begins with the commitment and desire to change within the individual person. If people are not transformed in their hearts, and do not personally commit fully to love, the movement to build a common culture based on the primacy of love would degenerate into an ugly fascism of the righteous do-gooders. The importance of those talking the talk, and walking the walk cannot be overstated. Those who oppose the Civilization of Love will look for hypocrisy and contradiction to discredit the

> "You are my brother
> and we are the children
> of one universal Holy Spirit.
> You are my likeness
> for we are prisoners of two
> bodies formed of one clay.
> You are my companion on
> the road of life
> And my helper in the
> understanding of a truth
> concealed beyond the clouds
> You are my brother
> and I love you.   Kahlil Gibran

the Civilization of love

movement. Alongside courage and perseverance, integrity and humility are crucial traits in authentic activists.

Patterns of fearful thought and behavior do not merely fall away in the presence of truth; but human beings CAN change their minds, their hearts, their lives, and their world. While none of reach perfection, the commitment to personal change is central. Engaged in the process of personal growth we come to realize that we are no better than anybody else. The self-absorption epidemic, that blocks the flow of love in life affects all of us, even those of us committed to love. Everything easily becomes filtered through the lens of "What about ME?"

> "Don't look for big things, just do small things with great love.... The smaller the thing, the greater must be our love."
> -Mother Teresa

Before we build the Civilization of Love for others, before we challenge others in leadership to change systemic structures that limit human growth and perpetuate human suffering, we have to allow ourselves to be changed that we might first live in the Civilization of Love ourselves. This is not saying we attain personal perfection and then we try to change others. This belief system keeps its believers passive, since none of us will ever be perfect enough.

> "Everyone can be great because everyone can serve."
> Martin Luther King

Recognizing our imperfections includes recognizing that every day we hurt people intentionally or through neglect. Our participation in, our refusing to question or to acquiesce to an unloving system leads to the pain and suffering or countless others. Every day, every moment of our lives, through our actions, we are either building or killing The Civilization of Love. By accepting personal re-

the Civilization of love

sponsibility; we do what we can for the world and its future by first committing ourselves to living our personal lives with as much love as we can before expecting the same from anyone else, including our leaders.

Real change cannot occur until we are willing to imagine and embrace going against the tide. It is countercultural to be content with your status in life, but letting go of attachment to money and power frees up something huge inside us. When we desire integrity more than anything else, the narcissism of the modern era perpetuated by social media is seen for the shallow waste of time and energy it is.

If we allow the tangible effects of the injustices of the world on real human beings to affect us in lasting ways, we grow in imagination and perseverance, and we will not settle for making an immediate impact for instant gratification and relieving our need to feel good. People and causes are not problems to be solved. The way of real progress is love through solidarity, engagement, respect, dignity, and relationship, or else the effect is further dehumanization, and there is probably nothing in life more discouraging than dehumanization done in the name of love. We passionately throw ourselves into making the difference each of us alone can make, the unique contribution to the Civilization of Love that no one else can. We work hard, and accept criticism and advice about what matters to us, willing to investigate deeply and gain information from below the surface. It's important that some of us specialize in specific areas and gain more than a superficial knowledge.

We act. We lose nothing by the refusal of others to love.
What are **you** doing to build the Civilization of Love?
What can you **do today**?

the Civilization of love

The Civilization of Love movement is social

In the absence of love in human affairs and at all levels, there is only war, and where there is war, in all its forms, there is always a conqueror, and a conquered, a master and a slave; a hammer and a nail, setting the stage for some form of oppression, exploitation, subjugation, and ultimately desire for revenge, all of which degrade both the conqueror and the conquered, and block the expression and development of true humanity. The Culture of Death is saturated with lies and deception, and society grows to prefer its comfort to the messiness of confrontation. Human discourse becomes polluted and human activity is damaged by the rhetoric of fear and hate. Human beings' refusal to love leads to their easy manipulation. The world self-destructs because of greed, ignorance, mismanagement and depletion of necessary natural and human resources.

The orgy of consumption of the world's resources poisons the fragile ecosystem. The lust for profits at any cost, leads to the accumulation of wealth at the expense of human existence and dignity. Urgency is required to protect human beings and the environment. Human beings are systematically degraded by the steady deterioration of human rights. Workers are enslaved by being over-worked and paid low wages.

Nations not corporations

In the global era, how will humans organize themselves for their greatest development? The evolving choice seems to be between the nation-state and the economic corporation. While it is unlikely that nation-states will completely wither away; it is clear that they have lost or given over huge power over to national and multinational corpo-

the Civilization of love

rations. Individual and allied nation states, not corporations, are the means for human organization in the world. All economic and social entities are subservient to the people, and to the primacy of love. Corporate and financial entities can never be the integrating force in society. They can never be allowed to be the most powerful systems on earth, because they have only one purpose: profit for their owners. They have no loyalty to the people and no motivation to the cause of love, since business profit at any cost flies in the face of any concern for what may be in the best interest of the development of the whole of humanity. Social development comes through the collective governance and not the private corporate/banking sector. Decisions must be made on the merit of what brings the greatest good into existence, not what is best for the few, as in corporate profits. Corporations or any other business enterprises must never be allowed in scope or power to supersede the power of peoples through their national governments and international bodies.

There has been a significant shift in the balance of power to economic corporations through government policy and significant mergers. In democracies, where people can have power to shape their society, these corporations are accountable to no one but themselves and their stockholders, and their accumulation of money, power and control over resources grows unimpeded. Economic entities such as banks and corporations must always be accountable to the will of the people. The best way to remind them of that is for people to use their economic power as consumers.

Neither corporations nor governments, must ultimately dictate the shape of the future. The integrating factor for human society is the dignity of the individual human person, and our collective humanity. All states, i.e. all so-

the Civilization of love

cieties exist for the security and development of their people. The era of human tribal warfare, in all its forms of murder and violence, human enslavement, exploitation, and oppression of the vulnerable by the wealthy and powerful has reigned for too long. The respect for and development of all human beings is paramount. The cultivation of human life through love is the future for humanity.

Social change is difficult

In developed affluent societies where the system is actually working for the benefit of most; massive change, except in times of crisis, is usually not welcome. As their little bit of wealth is swept away by incompetent or corrupt leaders, people simply find themselves working harder and longer to maintain what they have gotten used to.

> **Gandhi's Social Sins:**
> Wealth without work.
> Pleasure without conscience.
> Knowledge without character.
> Commerce without morality.
> Science without humanity.
> Worship without sacrifice.
> Politics without principle.
> Rights without responsibilities

In societies where there is great poverty, people are usually working so hard and long for their own survival, or to improve their family's living conditions that they don't have the time and energy to get involved in changing the system.

The great equalizer in every society is that rich, poor, or middle, everyone has been distracted and lulled to sleep with lies and the array of endless media entertainment and diversions designed to fill up every free waking moment.

The increased specialization in advanced societies can also be immobilizing. Even if people sense that something is terribly wrong and want a better world for themselves and their children, they feel that there must be

the Civilization of love

someone else more qualified than they are to do something about it.

The Civilization of Love requires personal **and** social responsibility. Human life can only advance when individual and collective choices are made to live in loving ways and stand up to the many forms of personal and social enslavement. People will always have the right to protect themselves from those who intend to harm them and their loved ones, and that includes from leaders who allow the destruction of the planet and human life.
In the social arena we employ both forms of love: charity and justice.
Charity: relief, the alleviation of suffering caused by man-made crises and natural disasters,
Justice: the development and empowering of people through opportunities such as training, loans, sharing resources.

The Civilization of Love movement is political

We would never run our lives the way we let our political leaders run our governments in our name. So why do we let them? We don't wait for the system to change first so we might live in the Civilization of Love. We also don't avoid activism to make systems behave in ways that reflect the highest values that humans are capable of. Change never comes from accommodating existing power structures that oppress, exploit, pollute, devour, deceive, enslave, repress and kill in order to make profit and maintain themselves. Change only comes through confronting them.

The comfort of the few has been made possible by the seizing and exploitation of the planet, with no concern for the common good, only for personal gain, for which

the Civilization of love

are employed war, propaganda, prisons, and creating pollution, oppression, exploitation, and poison of every kind. The world is broken and what global movement currently gives people a real choice? What movement acts as a counterweight to the tyranny of the empires, be they the corporate capitalist pseudo-democratic states, repressive totalitarian dictatorships and states, or fascist religious groups?

The result of having no alternative is despair and cynicism, and the withdrawal of the masses into their private little worlds, away from a system they believe they need, but hate.

> *"When I despair, I remember that all through history the way of truth and love have always won. There have been tyrants and murderers, and for a time, they can seem invincible, but in the end, they always fall. Think of it - always."* Mahatma Gandhi

Confronting tyrannical systems and leaders

We need to stop continually empowering and enabling the loveless system to dominate our collective affairs. As long as we accept its inevitability, settle for occasional crumbs, and buy into fear-mongering propaganda, we will be duped by one leader after another. Until we commit to living lives of love ourselves, we will accept that our leaders and our fellow human beings are not capable of loving either, and we compromise whatever integrity we have and worst of all pass on to our children a compromised reality.

So much of what passes for political debate in democracies consists of dueling fear-based ideologies, and so much of political activity is really just demonizing and fear-mongering. So much of governmental policy and action is for personal benefit and that of special interests. In other nations, time and again, men rise up against

the Civilization of love

despotic dictators who consider their countries their personal domain, only to become the same kind of tyrannical leaders ruthlessly accruing power and wealth for their own advantage. They fool no one as they allow their people to struggle while throwing them scraps and a steady flow of propaganda.

Those who commit their lives to love have a right and a responsibility to refuse to support leaders who use their power and position for the benefit of themselves and for the few. They have a right and responsibility to be able to vote for leaders who will commit their position and power to the cause of love and the forms it must take in their particular society and the world. People deserve the option of standing up for their belief that the collective group make it's decisions guided by love and the highest principles that they use to guide their personal lives.

> When evil men plot, good men must plan. When evil men burn and bomb, good men must build and bind. When evil men shout ugly words of hatred, good men must commit themselves to the glories of love. Where evil men would seek to perpetuate an unjust status quo, good men must seek to bring into being a real order of justice.   Martin Luther King Jr

The establishment and development of Civilization of Love political parties is crucial to any social, political and economic change. People have the right to elect leaders who put love first and demand they use love to manage our collective governance. Love deserves more than lip service, but when it comes to national and international discourse and policy, it doesn't even receive that. Leaders speak only of freedom, tribal pride, and economic prosperity. They do not even speak of love for the

the Civilization of love

citizens they lead, never mind others, and definitely not enemies.

We honor those who die in the name of national causes, those who nobly risk and sacrifice their lives for their fellow citizens; yet shamefully, we do not in their memory and honor commit to conducting our affairs in better, more loving ways. Following horrific wars people naively say "never again", yet soon, manipulated by the propaganda of incompetent leaders, cynically accept and therefore cooperate with the perceived necessity of an endless parade of warfare. Of course the existence and possibility of dangerous threat from outside borders and be real; but so often leaders seek to accumulate power by creating fear, convincing their people that the other side, which they have demonized to justify their violence, cannot be trusted, and that any tactic besides violent threats, confrontation, and retribution cannot be risked.

> *"The limitation of riots, moral questions aside, is that they cannot win and their participants know it. Hence, rioting is not revolutionary but reactionary because it invites defeat. It involves an emotional catharsis, but it must be followed by a sense of futility."* Martin Luther King, Jr.

Love is not weakness, it is ultimate strength. We are not naive utopians, we are hard workers who are building a new way of life, one decision, one action, one brick at a time. In shaping this Civilization of Love we are serving warning to the leaders of the world-- that love must come first, that things must change, and we are prepared to use any nonviolent method necessary to achieve that change. The people who believe in love are

the Civilization of love

coming to take the systems from fear-based leaders, at all levels, from the most local to the international.

Political parties

The Civilization of Love movement is bigger than politics, but we are social beings in unified systems, and politics is the way we do our business. Therefore political activity is required of those in the Civilization of Love movement. Major political parties are attached to the establishment of the countries they operate in, and either not open to, or standing for, real change. They may also be ineffectual at implementing anything of substance, and definitely not on the level the Civilization of Love calls for. Infiltration of and involvement in existing political parties may be a noble cause for some, but it would not be surprising to discover that real opportunity to represent the Civilization of Love agenda will not exist.

Caution must be taken that Civilization of Love parties and political candidates are not co-opted and aligned with other parties, groups or individuals seeking to include them in coalitions that ultimately compromise and do not serve the Civilization of Love agenda. The Civilization of Love is not a political organization, but an **international movement**. It will have political implications as Civilization of Love organizations develop in every nation since citizens in every nation have a right and responsibility to stand up demanding that their governments conduct their business in ways that create more love in the world and not less.

There are no illusions or guarantees that joining an on-line community and forming a Civilization of Love party will in and of itself change anything, but those actions are significant in that minimally they are effective ways to bring people together, and their growth in numbers will indicate to leaders where their people are at and what is expected

the Civilization of love

of them. Political activity in democracies, with all their imperfections are where there is at least some hope for the will of the people to be implemented.

The potential is very real for Civilization of Love parties to be infiltrated with those who will attempt to sow discord and create embarrassment. While there certainly will be disagreements on how to best create the most love, be on the lookout for those whose only purpose seems to be divisive. Discern people's motives by their actions, rather than their words. Don't be afraid of serious or severe actions, and forbid anything that is violent. Power must be confronted, and we are up against incredible power.

The grassroots is where real growth occurs. Consultation and action at the local level is what works, not the imposing of solutions from above. The Civilization of Love movement is a combination of increased personal commitment to love, and a collective transformation of human systems to reflect the commitment to love. No nation, no international body has ever said that love is the principle that guides their collective action. Is that acceptable to you? Do you really want to say to future generations "sorry, this is the best we could do, and likely the best you'll ever do?" And to the young who are reading this, if it disgusts you how little is done to make the world better, then I beg you to use your youthful zeal and stamina and take a stand. I also implore you to stay true when the sys-

> *When evil men plot, good men must plan. When evil men burn and bomb, good men must build and bind. When evil men shout ugly words of hatred, good men must commit themselves to the glories of love. Where evil men would seek to perpetuate an unjust status quo, good men must seek to bring into being a real order of justice.*   Martin Luther King Jr

the Civilization of love

tems of the world are passed into your hands. Generations of idealistic youth have come and gone. Once they discover the real workings of the world and have to navigate their way through them to insure their survival, all kinds of principles and values get compromised or discarded.

This is why a true movement for change must also include those who have much to lose when the fear and greed-based system is overhauled. The lack of a clear love alternative allows everyone in the affluent world to maintain their comfort. If it is never proposed or promoted their enemies can never say, they have an alternative, but they reject it, so they do wish to exploit us, they could choose differently. The absence of a love agenda allows everyone to keep playing the game the way they always have, pretending there is no alternative. No real change happens until love is the way of proceeding.

Leadership
Who should lead?

Throughout history human beings have experimented with many different forms of leadership including: royalty, military, democratically elected, legally proficient, financially successful, and dictatorship. People have chosen leaders on their ability to charm, swagger, and boost their self esteem and confidence. Leaders have risen to the top based on their personality, organizational skills, past accomplishments, and ability to read the deepest needs and fears of their people. Others have grabbed for power using sheer manipulation and violence. At every level of social governance, *illegitimate* leaders and governments fail to recognize that integrity, transparency and service are essential to true leadership, and not popularity or personal benefit for themselves and their associ-

the Civilization of love

ates. Nobility of character, and the commitment to loving service, and not power for its own sake, is the essence of true leadership.

Pre-conditions such as training, economic class, political experience, knowledge of the law, military prowess or social connection are not as necessary in the leaders that must evolve to implement the Civilization of Love. The primary precondition is the faithfulness to love as the foundation of all personal and collective activity. Leaders must no longer be those who beat their chests the hardest, most effectively intimidate, manipulate or oppress the members of their own tribe, or appear most menacing to other tribes.

Leaders must possess competence, and also a desire to love, and a level of strength and character that embodies the most noble of ideals, even when their tribe might be lagging behind. Leaders at the local, national, and international levels, in every social, economic and political setting are obligated to carry out their duties of representing us and handling our affairs in our name, adhering to the principle and practice of love instead of systematic enslavement.

Legitimate leadership uses power to serve. No one has the right to run a country if they do not have a global vision of how their people will contribute to the elevation of all of humanity, instead of defining their people in terms of monetary value, or economic usefulness.

> "True leadership is about service."
> Pope Francis

Vision is not enough, leaders need to know how to get things done, having knowledge and experience with organizing people, and managing systems, especially the ability to communicate and facilitate.

the Civilization of Love

Political action can include:
*refusing to vote for anybody who is not committed to building the Civilization of Love
*making yourself available to serve in a leadership capacity even if you are relatively politically inexperienced
*providing resources for the campaigns of candidates committed to the Civilization of Love.
*insisting that nations and the global community be organized in ways that treats people as human beings and not just intelligent animals.
*joining or starting a Civilization of Love political party in your community, state, or country
*using the Civilization of Love website to inform and organize

We have had far too many politicians who play on people's hopes for a better life, wave the flag and the holy books and symbols, but have no love. We are no longer lulled to sleep. We are sick of the lies and the suffering they cause. We reject those who attempt to make us feel hopeless by either cynically promoting a loveless agenda or worse, tug at our heartstrings, the part of us that longs for a better way of life than what humans have developed up to this point, and then betray us once elected.

> *"To be truly radical is to make hope possible than than despair convincing."*
> Raymond Williams

  Regardless of anyone's religious or philosophical belief system; the common ground that the Civilization of Love establishes is that love is the only hope that humanity ever has. We see this truth evident in our individual lives, and it is time to recognize and insist that it must be the practice in our collective governance.
  Leaders can justify not having a responsibility to act in a loving manner when their people don't demand it.

the Civilization of love

Expressing our voices through the Civilization of Love movement, website, political parties, and other means that will evolve, are ways of voicing our insistence and resistance.

Those who hold elected positions conduct the affairs we have elected them to, are obligated to loving action; to do the most good for the most people with what resources are available, while refusing to accept or implement violence in all its forms: physical, economic and environmental.

A warning: Human beings generally dislike drastic change. We continually fall for leaders who make us feel good by promising that they will make things better, while lacking the vision to do the things, to make the changes that actually can make things better, by rebuilding institutions on the principle of love. Leaders who promise real change, but then make only incremental improvements are not the solution. Total commitment to building, and maintaining a loving system is the necessary unifying force, or else humanity is merely rearranging furniture on a ship that is sinking.

> "The first test of a truly great man is his humility. By humility I don't mean doubt of his powers or hesitation in speaking his opinion, but merely an understanding of the relationship of what he can say and what he can do." — John Ruskin

Taking action

"Hozho nahasdlii" is a Navajo phrase that conveys the restoration of beauty, balance and oneness. It exemplifies the purpose of the Civilization of Love movement. What matters more than anything is not what you believe; but *"what you are willing to do?"*

the Civilization of Love

Because human beings do not usually take action unless they are in danger, those who believe in the Civilization of Love, without becoming fear-mongering or alarmists, must clearly depict the danger that we are all in if we do not change.

Will you take responsibility for where you live, your home, neighborhood, organization, community, country, world?
There is no real progress without cost, but with sacrifice, much can be done. Citizens committed to the law to love obviously never attempt to create change with violence and never return violence with more.

We take specific individual and collective action:
*Living simply; choosing to let go of what is unnecessary beyond basic needs.
*Examining what the organizations and companies we are associated with, work for and do business with, stand for, and being willing to impact on them in a transforming way if necessary. As long as we are silent, we are compliant and complicit.
*Spreading the Civilization of Love message and movement, especially to international connections. Always remember there's more of us than we might think.
*Taking individual action, being a beacon and light and hope by the way we conduct our lives caring for those around us, working as much for their well-being as for our own.
*Working at every level of organization from local government, schools, churches, and businesses, to the national, to the global, to insure that the actions of those institutions follow the principles of love and are working for change, utilizing many ways to affect change ranging from protest, to voting, to artistic expression.

the Civilization of love

*Getting to know our political representatives, their decisions and their moral compass. Letting them know of our convictions and holding them accountable. It is easy to blame the leaders; but if leaders do not know that the people they represent demand that they operate their affairs in their name guided by principles of love and justice, then they can feel justified in maintaining the status quo with no impetus to move in that riskier loving direction. Rare is the political and social leader who sees what needs to be done and without popular support courageously moves his or her people in that direction.

> "Always renew the common horizon of hope that makes a good journey,"
> ~ Pope Francis

We are not simply demanding anything else of others "YOU out there should take care of ___".
This is a movement that is about personal responsibility.
We overwhelm the Culture of Death by spreading love.
We challenge the propaganda, lies, and illusions with telling the truth.
We defy the hideous and mundane with the creation of beauty.
We confront corruption, injustice, and evil with goodness and justice.

Members of the Civilization of Love movement are willing to:
1-commit to the law of love as the guide for their personal life.
2-identify themselves as members of this movement, on the website, and within their families, circle of friends, and society.

the Civilization of love

3-make a difference in their social, work, educational settings to build them into organisms that facilitate the civilization of love.
4-look within and around to discern if they or someone they know should step up and be available to serve in a position of leadership.
5-support candidates at the city, state, national levels who are committed to the Civilization of Love agenda.

Is it enough?

When have you felt most fully alive in this lifetime? You may recall the moments of true exhilaration and fulfillment in life that were experiences of love:

> "The meek shall inherit the earth."
> Jesus

-Someone doing something for you that they did not have to
-The joy of doing something for another spontaneously or anonymously
-Making love
-The transformation of an ugly situation by one person's self-sacrificing love
-The pure adoration of an infant or little child
-The selfless joining together for a greater good, or to help and relieve suffering during a crisis or disaster
-Our own sacrificing for the common good rather than exploiting for personal gain

We all know that the only lasting happiness in this life comes with giving to others, not taking from them. Can we allow these memories of concrete experiences, and our intuitive knowing to empower our daring to dream of and create a way of life and a world where there is far more love than there is now?

the Civilization of Love

No Illusions

- **Human inertia** is an issue and may be the biggest obstacle to building a new world. There is a great difficulty in motivating people to change unless they perceive immanent danger.
- **Human need** for organizations and systems. They exist so that we don't slip into will anarchy and chaos.
- **Human belief** in privilege carried by those doing the difficult and stressful work of managing the systems.
- **Human desire** for nice things for ourselves and those we care about, seeking to attain them even if they may belong to another.
- **Human propensity** for violence, even murder, in order to attain what we believe we need to survive and thrive.
- **Human resilience** is remarkable, giving us the ability to rebound from disaster. Two world wars, nuclear weapons, the Cold War, and the terror of perpetual war and conflict still have not forced humanity to declare "No more."

It is important to acknowledge the reality of human behavior, but none of these factors are not inevitable in the course of human individual and collective affairs. It is unnecessary and degrading to cynically embrace a lower way of behaving in the face of a dominant lower level of consciousness. We need not allow others to drag us or our society down. The Civilization of Love *is* radical, subversive, **and dangerous**. The only thing *more* dangerous is continuing down the path that we have been (and are currently on).

If you remain doubtful about the path proposed in this book, I ask you to go to the first child you see. Look them in the eye and tell them: "This is it. This world you

the Civilization of love

see around you, this is the best we can do, and it's all you will ever be able to look forward to. Sorry."
Does that feel wrong?
Of course it does. You just don't do that. You never tell the children "this is as good as it gets."
The Civilization of Love is not a dream; it is real, and as to when it will be manifested in physical reality on the scale of collective human life on this planet, will be limited only by the lack of courage of human beings.
Many know the truth, but accept, "It just has to be this way."
No it doesn't.

Beyond victims and slaves
There are 2 negative ways of adapting to the culture of death:
1-Slave- To do nothing, deny reality, and accept the mentality and status of slave of the system and those who run it. The slave mentality puts the responsibility on someone else. Personal irresponsibility feeds the cycle of social disintegration.
2- Victim- This mentality and behavior consists of looking for someone to blame and lash out at and punish those running the system. The victim mindset leads to violence, revenge, in many forms that never lead to a positive change.

An allegiance to a moral code that is absent in the system, makes it impossible to defend, work with, stand with, and acquiesce to that system. In this respect slavery is a choice. Resistance, the refusal to be paid off, bought out, and owned, and taking personal action for the improvement of the world are the necessary alternative to slavery and victimhood. We can refuse to cooperate, to feed the machine, to be part of its apparatus. Every generation has a choice to make:

the Civilization of love

1-It can either be merely another generation that failed to love more than to fear. Just another generation that will be forgotten, ignored, or even reviled for consuming itself with it's petty affairs and grievances, while lacking the courage and stamina to truly make a new world.

2- Or be the generation that was the one who dared find the ways to build what human beings have held in their hearts and souls for all time, the dream that a better way of living together as human beings was not only possible, but their destiny.

The dream of every generation

On the deepest level, every generation is driven by the impetus that the next generation to follow them should have it better than they did. Despite glimmers of hope that exist in every corner of the earth, where people are already sacrificing to bring love into the world, we still witness goodness slipping away. We know in our souls that if something big doesn't happen, the world we are leaving our children will not only **not** be better than the way we found it, it will be infinitely worse.

It is time to ask ourselves honestly:
*Who am I really, and what am I doing here?
*Am I contributing to the establishment of a Civilization of Love? Am I overtly involved in expanding the Culture of Death, or do I covertly have complicity in it by my apathy or inaction?
*Will I dare be part of the greatest of human adventures?
*How will those future generations to follow me look back at me, and how I lived, and the suffering and damage I allowed on my shift?
*What will I be able to tell my children and grandchildren when they ask "when the world was in pain, and the Civilization of Love was first being built, what did YOU do?

the Civilization of Love

Building the Civilization of Love is about finding new ways to empower us more, to curb our worst instincts and cultivate our best ones, so that we can live together in ways that nurture and express our humanity.
It is Not for the faint of heart!

You should have no illusions about what it will take for the Civilization of Love to be born. There is a cost for living justly, generously, sacrificially; for surrendering to what love calls you to do. Those who will build it by bringing about change in any arena of life, big and small, must be prepared to pay a price. The birth pains endured from bringing the Civilization of Love into being will be on a level that we have never seen before. Self-sacrifice is never to be sought after in a masochistic way, but rather accepted and embraced as part of the process. When it is clear that love is becoming the order of the day, those who have a great deal to lose will do everything in their power to destroy this movement and anyone in it who attempts to break their stranglehold of power. This is about confronting great power. Systems have locked in, people have been bought and sold, and nobody willingly walks away from what serves their advantage without a fight.

There will be attempts to destroy the message by discrediting and ostracizing the messengers through character assassination, embarrassment, and ruination of reputation. It can be insured that every mistake ever made will come to light.

Expect to be the brunt of many a joke.
Expect to be declared naive, foolishly optimistic, oblivious or insane.
Expect to be told to grow up and get real.
Expect you may be rejected by friends, even family
Expect that every mistake you have ever committed will
    be discovered, exposed and distributed everywhere

the Civilization of love

attempting to depict you as a dangerous fraud. Expect that you may even be socially or financially destroyed or even killed.

Strength
But love is stronger, infinitely so, and it is worth giving everything for. Building the Civilization of Love, loyally standing with the weak, poor, marginalized, oppressed exacts a price, and so requires incredible modern day courage, humility, integrity, and strength. It would be negligent to not mention that the cultivation of your inner life, on whatever path you might be on, is crucial.

Everyone who agrees with the premise of this book will have to ask themselves a question: does the idea of changing the world by building a Civilization of Love merely intrigue you, or do you really want to personally build it? It is important to remember that without love, nothing *really* changes. All that ever happens is faces change, and perhaps some damage control is accomplished. How does the world actually change?

Many believe in love, being willing to act on beliefs is totally different.

Love is Action
* Make something good happen every day.
* Build an action community, coming and working together.
* Work quietly, without seeking power or glory.
* Start small and natural.

the Civilization of love

> "Humanity grows more and more intelligent, yet there is clearly more trouble and less happiness daily. How can this be so? It is because intelligence is not the same thing as wisdom...
> When a society misuses partial intelligence and ignores holistic wisdom, its people forget the benefits of a plain and natural life. Seduced by their desires, emotions, and egos, they become slaves to bodily demands, to luxuries, to power and unbalanced religion and psychological excuses. Then the reign of calamity and confusion begins. Nonetheless, some people can awaken during times of turmoil to lead others out of the mire. But how can the one liberate the many? By first liberating his own being. He does this nor by elevating himself, but by lowering himself. He lowers himself to that which is simple, modest, true; integrating it into himself, he becomes a master of simplicity, modesty, truth. Completely emancipated from his former false life, he discovers his original pure nature, which is the pure nature of the universe."   Lao Tzu   2500 yrs. ago

* Seek understanding and guidance.
* Lead with action rather than words.
* Be innovative, generous and creative with time, energy, and resources.
* Speak truth to power and challenge the dominant paradigm.
* Write letters and articles for media.
* Organize or participate in peaceful demonstrations to confront corruption, injustice, and evil.
* Live, work, and play with integrity.

> "Many small people, who in many small places do many small things, can alter the face of the world."
> Graffiti from the Berlin Wall

Promote the Civilization of Love:
* Word of mouth.
* Start a blog.
* Order discount copies of books for your friends and family.

the Civilization of love

* Log onto the Civilization of Love website.
* Make this movement go viral, tweet, post, etc.
* Use your technological, artistic, or organizational talents to get the message out.
* Host a discussion group, I am willing to meet with people who have read this book to discuss their thoughts and plans of action.

> "Never doubt that a small group of thoughtful, committed citizens can change the world. Indeed, it is the only thing that ever has."
> – Margaret Mead

Water in the desert

We will not force our children to live this way. The way we are doing things is not working. The human suffering, the destruction done to our home, the diminishing development of human life is not acceptable. To continue it is to shame ourselves in front of our children and all of human history. Do we have the determination to confront and turn around the anarchy and moral collapse that has resulted from irresponsibility, selfishness, and behaving as though choices have no consequences? Even greater tyranny and suffering are around the corner if we do not.

The world is increasingly a desert of despair, loneliness, and suffering. You can be an instrument to bring it to life. There are rains of healing and refreshment waiting to pour down, but there is not enough love in the world. And that can change. It starts with you.

Will you make your life an oasis:
* Diligently being willing to confront your own selfishness
* Courageously living a loving life in the face of the lies.
* Seeking needed vision to shape our common reality and institutions with love

the Civilization of love

Together our rejection of fear, hatred, and greed, and our commitment to love will lead to a flourishing of life, replacing the barren wasteland.

Here's a great secret: if you change the world with love, it changes YOU. The greatest result from committing to build the Civilization of Love is the way it will shape everyone's lives, especially the young. As they grow in a loving environment, their vision will be shaped, their decisions framed by the awareness that they are part of the creation of a new world of beauty and grace, and not a culture that is degrading and subhuman.

We've had an Age of Reason.
We've had an Information age.
It's time for an age of reason and information serving Love.
Everything else has been tried.
It's time to build a Civilization of Love.
It is time to make all things balanced, beautiful, and one.

Epilogue
The Hopi Elders Speak

We Are the Ones We've Been Waiting For
You have been telling the people that this is the Eleventh Hour.
Now you must go back and tell the people that this is The Hour.
And there are things to be considered: Where are you living? What are you doing?
What are your relationships? Are you in right relation?
Where is your water? Know your garden.
It is time to speak your Truth.
Create your community. Be good to each other.
And do not look outside yourself for the leader. This could be a good time!
There is a river flowing now very fast. It is so great and swift that there are those who will be afraid. They will try to hold on to the shore. They will feel they are being torn apart, and they will suffer greatly.
Know the river has its destination. The elders say we must let go of the shore, push off into the middle of the river, keep our eyes open, and our heads above the water.
See who is in there with you and celebrate.
At this time in history, we are to take nothing personally.

the Civilization of love

Least of all, ourselves.
For the moment that we do, our spiritual growth and journey comes to a halt.
The time of the lone wolf is over. Gather yourselves!
Banish the word struggle from your attitude and your vocabulary.
All that we do now must be done in a sacred manner and in celebration.
We are the ones we've been waiting for. —The Elders Oraibi   Arizona Hopi Nation

"We must build a Civilization of Love or we will have no civilization at all. It is love that will save our world."
Martin Luther King Jr.

The Civilization of Love is a call to action on an unprecedented level. A world animated by the power, and beauty of love is not a dream. It is our destiny.

A supplement on the connection of Christian beliefs with the contents of this book is available. Supplementary materials on the correlation of scientific disciplines, religious teachings, spiritual paths, philosophies with the Civilization of Love are welcome.

You are invited to join, enjoy, and contribute to the Civilization of Love movement website:

TheCivilizationOfLove.com

the Civilization of love

Tony Bellizzi is founder and director of The Hope for the Children Foundation, and is available to speak about and build with anyone, anywhere about "The Civilization of Love".
718-479-2594, Facebook,
Email: tony@TheCivilizationofLove.com
All proceeds from the sale of this book, other products, or speaking engagements are used for the development of this cause, and for charity.

Order Form
"The Civilization of Love" is also available in hard copy @Amazon, and e-book format through Amazon and i-tunes.

NOTE: "Hope for the Children" is a charity sponsored by the author and is not associated with "The Civilization of Love" movement. Amounts are suggested donations to help provide charitable assistance and opportunities for those in need.
Please include within order $3.00 postage and handling within the US.   (International postage extra)

"The Civilization of Love" book
___$10.00 each
___20 or more $8.00 each
___100 or more $5.00 each

Make Checks out to: " Hope for the Children"
mail to: 9021 Springfield Blvd.
                      Queens Village NY 11428

Name_____

Address _____

City, State, Zip_____